CW00517438

The Book Writer

Fast Guide on How to Best Write a Book in Less Than a Week: For Beginners

© **Copyright 2020 - All rights reserved.**

The content contained within this book may not be reproduced, duplicated or transmitted without direct written permission from the author or the publisher.

Under no circumstances will any blame or legal responsibility be held against the publisher, or author, for any damages, reparation, or monetary loss due to the information contained within this book, either directly or indirectly.

Legal Notice:

This book is copyright protected. It is only for personal use. You cannot amend, distribute, sell, use, quote or paraphrase any part, or the content within this book, without the consent of the author or publisher.

Disclaimer Notice:

Please note the information contained within this document is for educational and entertainment purposes only. All effort has been executed to present accurate, up to date, reliable, complete information. No warranties of any kind are declared or implied. Readers acknowledge that the author is not engaging in the rendering of legal, financial, medical or professional advice. The content within this book has been derived from various sources. Please consult a licensed professional before attempting any techniques outlined in this book.

By reading this document, the reader agrees that under no circumstances is the author responsible for any losses, direct or indirect, that are incurred as a result of the use of information contained within this document, including, but not limited to, errors, omissions, or inaccuracies.

Table of Contents

Introduction

Writing a book must have been a goal for every writer at some point in their lives. If you're reading this book, it is definitely one of your strongest desires. But we know that writing a book is easier said than done. You simply cannot open your laptop and start writing. Or, you are just not motivated enough.

You've either been delaying it out of laziness or aren't confident enough to actually get the work done. But what if we said that you can finish your book in less than a week, while keeping the quality you anticipated? Yes, it is definitely possible. All you need is 6 days, a solid plan, and a little bit of confidence.

However, you will have to refrain from all kinds of social activities for these 6 days. Also, do not take up any new projects until you have finished with this one. It might seem a bit absurd and difficult to write a book in less than a week, especially if you are a newbie, but it is definitely possible. So, as a brief overview, your next 6 days will look something like this:

Day 1: Make a plan (self-assessment, brainstorming ideas, and dividing your word count)

Day 2: Research and outline chapters

Day 3, 4, 5: Begin writing

Day 6: Finishing up and editing

The following chapters will provide a realistic overview of writing a book according to the number of days you have. This guide will make sure that you are maintaining quality, getting your messages across, and finishing on time. Read on to begin finishing your dream project.

Chapter One: Day 1 - Make a Plan

Your first day into the project is extremely crucial as it will form the basis for your book. Needless to say, the foundation should be strong in any project. You will take the first day to formulate your plan. This will keep things in order and help you to finish your project in time.

The first day will involve finishing up basic but necessary tasks in order to begin writing your book. This will include conducting a personal assessment test, brainstorming ideas for your main subject, and dividing your word count for the rest of the days of the project. This will give you a definite head start for this project and motivate you to begin working on it.

Self-Assessment

Assessing yourself will give you an idea about why you want to write this book. 'Why' is the keyword here. Do you want to finally introduce yourself as an author? Do you have a strong message that you need people to know? Do you want to do it as a tactic for brand growth and marketing? Whatever the reason is, this 'why' will give you enough motivation to finish your project and get you going during lethargic hours.

Brainstorming Ideas

Unless you already have a book idea, you need to brainstorm and come up with a solid plot and subject for your book (depending on your genre). Your plot will determine whether your book is interesting or not.

If you are still unsure about the subject, you can follow this exercise.

Make a list of things that you are good at. Whether it's cooking, painting, or playing sports, list the tasks that you can master. It is not just confined to your talents; you can also jot down your skills as your former or current profession - a stockbroker, a teacher, a therapist, etc. This will help you to choose a topic for your non-fiction book, unless you have already decided on a topic. While you are at it, choose a topic or subject that you can easily write without conducting thorough research. This is why we are listing the topics that you have experience or expertise in. You should also contemplate the questions that your friends or close acquaintances often ask you about. Do they often come to you for relationship advice? Or do they ask you about real estate? Reflect on the subjects and you will be able to come up with a concrete topic to write about.

This exercise will help to determine the topics that you are most comfortable with. Take a look at the list, prioritize according to the easiest subjects, and select the one that will take minimum research and maximum interest.

Dividing your Word Count

A fiction novel usually consists of a word count ranging on average between 20,000 words to 50,000 words. Since you are a beginner, let's say that you are writing a book that includes a total word count of 25,000 words. Even though this will be a short novella, you will still attract readers as people seem to have less attention and reading span nowadays. The word count of your book won't matter much as long as you are successful in delivering the message. Readers, especially those who are trying to get back into reading, also prefer short reads as they are easier to finish. So, you are good to go. You can also increase your word count if your story demands.

The truth is, a smart man is not one who reads more pages than others. He is one who reads 10 pages and obtains the same amount of information instead of reading 100 pages of repetitive data. He saves time and gains knowledge simultaneously. So, don't worry about your word count. Stick to what your subject demands, whether it's a short book or a long one. Hence, the length of your book should be the least of your concerns. It is only important to fix the length and final word count to divide your time accordingly and get the work done on time.

Now, unless you are an expert novel writer or an author who has had experience in book-writing for a few years now, writing 25,000 words in a few days might seem a bit unattainable. However, it is not impossible. All you have to do is smartly divide the total number of words according to the number of days you have.

Say, you have 6 days to write a book. Your first and second day will go into assessment, research and chapter outlines as well as coming up with a title. You will need a half or the entire 6th day to edit your book. So this leaves us with a total of 3 to 3.5 days to actually write the book. This will give you a target of around 7500 words per day. If you target 8000 words per day, you will have more time to edit and revise your book on the 6th day. It will also depend on your writing speed. If you are a fast typist, you can get more work done in less time. But if you are slow, make sure that you leave enough room to reach the final word count. For instance, if you can type around 50 words per minute, you can get a whopping 3000 words done in one hour. Assuming that you are a beginner, this target is a bit difficult to achieve. It's not demotivation. We are just being realistic. Calculate your word count and divide according to the number of days you have.

You can also start writing on your 2nd day, if you manage to finish your research and outline your chapters on time.

You will have to work for at least 9 to 10 hours in a day to reach your word count, so be prepared for it. Your usual office hours last for around 9 hours, so consider it as a day-job. This will come down to 3500-4000 words in 4 to 5 hours, melting it to 700 to 900 words per hour. It's easily doable. However, make sure that you do not procrastinate or waste time so that you finish your word count for the day. This is just an example of an estimated word count. You can, of course, outline and divide your word count depending on your topic and plot. Just make sure that you have the drive and discipline to attain your goal in the following days.

Chapter Two: Day 2 - Research and Outline Chapters

Research is a vital step to ensure that the facts and sentences you write in your book are true and accurate. You need to dedicate almost an entire day to research about the facts you know and the ones that you don't. A solid research base is necessary to achieve authenticity and validity. Now, we are not talking about conducting a research assessment on the levels of Dan Brown, but you definitely need a strong fact check, especially if you are dealing with non-fiction.

Once you are done with the research and have gathered enough sources, it is time to outline the main chapters. By fleshing out chapters, you will no longer have a massive book to write. Your ultimate goal will be to finish these chapters seamlessly. And that can only be done if you have an outline of your chapters ready. You will also have a clear idea of what kind of content will go in which chapter, which will make things easier for you.

You can follow this suggested exercise to make things easier. This will definitely help you outline your chapters in no time. This method is called the 20-minutes technique.

1. Take a notepad, pen, and a timer or your mobile phone and set it for 10 minutes.

2. You need to think about the 6 to 10 messages that are crucial for your book. Ask yourself - what are the main points that my readers must know from reading my book?

3. Think and write these messages down until the timer goes off. Stop when the time is up.

4. The points that you jotted down will form your main chapters. You can polish the titles later.

5. Set the timer for 10 minutes again and now think about the key outcomes for each chapter. Write them down. This will also give you a brief idea about your sub-chapters or sub-titles if you plan to include them.

6. Once those 10 minutes are up, you will have the outline of your main chapters along with the main objectives and outcomes that you need to extract from each chapter.
You see, it's so easy. Whether it is fiction or nonfiction, this exercise works well with any genre. While it works the best with non-fiction books, you can also use the same plan to craft novellas. The process and outlining will be the same; you might just have to put in some more time and effort to outline your characters and plot. Since non-fiction books hold more information and less creativity, outlining such books is much easier as compared to fiction books. All you have to do is think about the information you need to deliver and smartly segregate the topics accordingly. The chapters should lead in a logical progression until the message and necessary information is delivered adequately.

It will also give you an opportunity to explore all possibilities of your book and give you a good head start. You will gain enough confidence to begin writing and finish it on time. If you've been thinking about writing and finishing this book for a while now, this exercise will finally give you an insight as to how your book will look at the end. With the tight timeline of just 20 minutes, you are not only finalizing your ideas on paper and committing to them, but you are also saving a lot of time to actually get other tasks done (given you only have 6 days to finish writing your book).

Apart from outlining your chapters, you will also have to create a profile of your characters if you are working on fiction. This profile will determine the main characteristics that you need to add and emphasize. It will also keep you aware about the consistency that you need to maintain throughout the book (unless your character undergoes a massive change within the plot). Character development and outlining is necessary because if you don't, it will show. Your readers are cheated if you fail to grow your characters throughout the book.

Let us take a few examples of compelling characters and see what they have in common. Atticus Finch, Harry Potter, Jane Eyre, and similar literature characters. All these characters have shown a potential development and growth throughout the books, which strengthens the novels. No character, no plot. As simple as that. If you are stuck with the character outlining, you can refer to this exercise:

1. **Define your characters** - protagonists, antagonists, courageous, dishonest. The characters should have distinguishable traits, which will define them, and your readers will be able to construct an image of them accordingly. This can be done by introducing the main characters early in your book and defining them before the main plot begins. Also, give them names. Describe your characters with a physical appearance, their hair color, height, skin color, etc.

2. **Attach a history or a backstory to your main characters**. How has the character evolved? What was his past? Where was he born? Where did he grow up? Who is his family? What are his goals? What does he like or dislike? You can follow along the path of questions like these. Dig deep. Tell your reader who your main character truly is.

3. **Make your characters 'human'**. It is more believable if you present your character with human traits, desires, and flaws. It is easier for your readers to identify and relate to them.

4. **Meanwhile, don't stop at portraying him as a hero**. Sure, he has flaws, but he is the main character for a reason. While his subtle flaws can be ignored, his heroic qualities should allow him to conquer his fears and fight for justice. Basically, make sure that your character's traits captivate your readers.

5. **You can add subtle nuances** of your own life and personal experiences to add depth to your character and story. This will give you the freedom to explore the story and make it more believable for your readers.

Do not forget to think about the title of your book. It should be catchy enough to attract a reader's attention. Even though they say, "Don't judge a book by its cover", we don't want to take any chances, do we? It is not necessary to finalize a title just yet. It's possible that you might come across a brilliant title in the middle of writing your book. Take your time with the title and come up with a strong name.

While you are at it, you might also want to finalize the look of your book cover, especially if you are planning to self-publish it. If you have any artwork that you are fascinated by or any particular concept in your mind, you can look for the relevant design on various websites or buy a photograph from stock sites. While this isn't a necessary task for you, it can really make a great impact on the overall look of your book. You can also try free tools like Canva, especially if you are not a designer or an artist. It will provide free templates that will be highly suitable for your book and that don't take more than 30 minutes to create.

While you need to outline your chapters and subtitles to give you a fair idea, you should also allow some flexibility in your writing. Whether you are a planner or a prevaricator, you need a schedule with a guided timeline along with some flexibility to make changes. You should know where you are going, but you should also allow some freedom to make changes that could heavily impact your story plot. After all, your plot is a major factor to decide whether your book will be a success or not. But make sure that you are sticking to the time frame and plan the changes accordingly.

Chapter Three: Day 3, 4, 5 - Begin Writing

Once you have your chapters with you, you can dedicate a certain number of words to each chapter. This will give you a realistic time frame and an opportunity to finish your book on time. You can also start writing on day 2, once you have finished outlining and dividing your chapters. It will give you more time to complete your book and enough thought process to get things right. Nothing can stop you if your muse hits you. The sooner, the better.

Ideally, on the 3rd day, you will start writing your book. Get your coffee machine ready and crack your knuckles because this will be a long day (among the many others ahead) for you. Do not slack and try to finish as much as you can on the first day so that you will have enough time to catch up on things later. The number of hours you save will also help to adjust or fix any unexpected changes midway and also give you enough time to edit. DO NOT PROCRASTINATE. You already have less time, do not waste more.

As we talked about earlier, reduce your social activity. Put your phone aside for the next 2 days. Consider this as a mission. You don't want to fail it, do you?

The most you can do is talk to a close friend or your partner who has an expertise in this field and ask them to keep a track of your account. This constant nudge from your acquaintances will also help to get work done on time. Or, consider making a bet with your colleague. You need to finish your book in time to win the bet. If you lose, you will be giving away a huge amount of money to your acquaintance. Is it enough motivation to push you to your limit? If you finish writing the designated number of words per day, you can easily win the bet. Not only will you have finished your 'impossible' project, but you will also save a lot of money.

You can use a timer to finish your designated word count within the time frame you have outlined. Try to get as many words done as possible on the first day. This will give you a jump start and a fair idea about the next chapters that you will be writing in the following days. It will also quicken your pace and virtually provide an outline for the content that is to be written next. When you start, you can time the minutes or hours you took to finish 500 hours, and dedicate your entire day accordingly. This will also include your breaks and resting time (perhaps a nap if you have enough time).

If this doesn't work, you can use apps like Pomodoro that will provide an automatic timer. How the Pomodoro technique works is - you will be given 25 minutes to write without any interruption. Once the first 25 minutes are up, you can take a 5-minute break. Continue working for another 25 minutes and repeat. You can take a break for 25 to 30 minutes once you complete four Pomodoros. Simple, isn't it? This will encourage you to work with the time you have.

And since you have your chapter names fully decided, it will be extremely easy to just finish your word count goal as you go on fleshing out chapters. Don't look at it like 'writing a book'; view it as 'finishing designated chapters'. This will make it easier for you. Start writing chapter 1 instead of the introduction. Come back to the introduction when you have finished writing the book as it will give you and the reader an overall idea of what the following chapters are about. You see, non-fiction writing is similar to giving speeches. You need to share your idea with your readers and try your best to get your message across.

Before you deliver the message, enlighten them on the message and make your readers aware and ready to ingest the message or information. Once you have done that, you repeat what you have already told them. It's quite simple; it's your introduction, your main chapters with the message and information, and conclusion.

Another simple tip to reach your word count is to dump words on the page. This is called stream of consciousness. You allow your brain and fingers to collaborate and write the information you already know. Let your mind vomit words and keep up the pace of your thoughts with your fingers typing as fast as they can. Do not worry about the quality of these sections. Let the words flow for now. When you have finished writing a certain part, you can go back and check it for grammatical errors or possible reshuffling of words.

While you are writing your book, make sure that you take enough breaks in between. Working continuously can saturate you and you will give up easily. Also, fix the number of working hours according to the time you prefer. Some people are early birds, while others are night owls.

Irrespective of whenever you work, just make sure that you are writing and completing your day's word count.

When it comes to the writing tool, it is advisable to use Google Docs over your good ol' MS Word. A lot of writers have made this silly mistake of jotting down their precious ideas and 'breakthrough' novel in MS Word or similar tools and then losing it over file disruption or accidentally deleting it. They had no backup and have lost months of hard work in a few minutes. A backup writing software or Google Docs will automatically save your work and you can continue writing your book from any device. This will also help when referring to and comparing your old notes or typed chapters with the new version.

Whenever you feel lazy or specifically feel like giving up, switch to easier chapters or parts of your books such as the prologue or the introduction. This will not require too much effort or brain picking and you can easily fill your word count.

If you have finished writing on day 5, it is time to format your book. Now, formatting isn't as easy as it sounds. You need to mindfully place your page numbers, table of contents, introduction, sections, and other important formatting elements within your book for it to make sense. You simply cannot copy-paste your chapters into a keynote template and expect the book to be formatted in a professional manner. Instead, you can use tools such as Reedsy that will help to format your book. If you have enough time, you can paste your chapters in this tool, which will format it into a book.

Chapter Four: Day 6 - Finishing Up and Editing

On the last day of your project, you need to finish writing your chapters. Make sure you finish as soon as possible so that you can give enough time to proofreading, editing, and fixing any kind of revisions you need to. Editing is an important step to remove extra fluff, add factors that you skipped, and to check and edit any spelling or grammatical errors. The last thing you need in your book is typos. Check and recheck for mistakes. A few readers love to point out mistakes and tend to focus on the grammar instead of the information. Even if your content is valuable, a simple mistake can ruin the entire reading experience. There are a lot of free online tools available that can help you with this. One such example is Grammarly. It is a simple tool that can help in pointing out mistakes that you might have overlooked.

After you finish your book, you should give it at least 4 to 5 hours of a break (more if possible) before you start editing. The plan will work in a more fitting way if you can complete the writing part on day 5. You might also want to edit your book in chunks or chapter-wise. Edit a certain number of words, take a break, have a coffee, and then go back to editing the next chunk after a while. Take it slowly but steadily. You are almost there; you can do it.

A lot of people underestimate the importance of editing. It actually demands putting in a lot of mental effort and requires your 100% attention. With the past 5 days being so hectic, you may try to ignore this step. Again, do not skip editing. It is what will make your book shine.

It's even better if you have an editor. You can also pay a freelance editor to check your work. There are plenty of freelancers available on websites such as Freelancer and Upwork. The money spent will be like an investment. A good editor will help you convert your book from better to the best and increase the potential of selling it, eventually making more sales.

If you can find and convince a friend or an acquaintance to read your work and give you honest reviews and suggestions, you will be able to understand an average reader's perspective. You would be so caught up in reading and writing your own work that you will not be able to distinguish the flaws in your book. A chapter that might seem perfect to you can be a bit confusing for your reader. Take your friends' suggestions, reflect on the mistakes, and try to correct as much as you can. If you have no one to read your work, take a nap or possibly a full night's sleep before you start editing it. Editing your book with a fresh mind and well rested eyes will surely help to point out the evident mistakes that were once hidden by your brain in writing mode. This break will also help your brain switch to editing mode.

To make sure that your book is absolutely perfect, consider re-revising and editing it again. This will surely point out mistakes that were ignored in the first attempt.

Once you are done editing it, you can consider self-publishing your book. There are three options for publishing.

1. Send this draft to big and small-scale publishing houses and wait for them to get back to you. Hundreds of writers send their drafts to numerous publishing houses on a daily basis so this could take time. But if you feel that your book has potential and stands out from the rest, you can definitely expect a call from one of those houses.

2. You can contact Organizations and companies that help in self-publishing. These companies take a certain amount of fee and pay for the production cost, graphic design, and they even have in-house editors. They take a percentage of the sales to cover the production cost and their profit. While this step demands a small sum with no guarantee of return of investment, it will certainly help to make your identity as a published author. It is beneficial for work opportunities as well. And if your book does well, a popular publishing company might take up your book

and decide to put it on the shelves; you never know.

3. You can publish it as an e-book within minutes, which will be available on Kindle for your readers to access easily.

Whatever option you choose, make sure that your book has valuable content and stands out from the rest. This will help to encourage more positive reviews, sales, and success. If you really want to make your mark in the writing niche at the earliest, you can also choose all options to publish your book, which will increase your chances.
Editing and publishing aren't the last stages of writing and finishing your book project. There is no point in writing an awesome book if your potential readers don't know about it at all. To do this, you need to promote and market your book. There are several low-cost ways of doing it without spending money on marketing agencies.

1. **Use social media platforms**. There are numerous free platforms that are constantly used by billions of users on a daily basis such as Instagram, Facebook, Snapchat, and Twitter. You can join Facebook groups or put up posts about your upcoming book. Ask your friends and relatives to share your posts to garner more attention.

2. **Conduct podcast interviews**. There are several bloggers who are constantly looking for writers or authors within specific niches.

Research and contact such content creators and conduct podcasts. This will help your book reach a larger audience.

3. **Organize a local book tour**. Places like bookstores, libraries, schools, and universities will attract a crowd that reads on a regular basis. Request these places to let you conduct book reading sessions, in exchange for services or a small fee. Give away free copies if you can.

4. **Create a mailing list** by exploring your contacts or luring people into signing up for freebies. To increase curiosity, you can also offer a small portion of your book, just like a movie trailer, but exclusive. Once you form your email list, send regular emails on updates and increase engagement. Make sure to not spam them and subtly interest them in buying your book.

Conclusion

After reading this book, you most certainly will have enough motivation to start working on your dream project. All you needed was a push and a realistic plan, which you have achieved by now. In the chapters above, you must have noticed the usage of the word 'motivation' in a few places. This word is key to keep you going and actually finish your project. Even if you have a concrete plan and a few days to finish writing your book, you still won't be able to do it if you lack motivation. Rewinding chapter 1, where you are asked to assess yourself - the 'why' will keep you motivated. This is especially necessary when you are facing issues midway such as procrastination, writers' block, or any other limitations. You will need some discipline to sail this boat. Just imagine how rewarding it will be at the end. Thinking about getting your book published is enough drive to keep going until you type the last word of your book.

Finishing your book in less than a week requires true commitment. Writing and publishing a book can make a good impression on your CV and help you gain recognition in the writing world. It also opens up several work opportunities within your domain. A side benefit is the extra income you can earn. If your book gets published and becomes a hit, you are bound to earn a lot of money and fame.

So, what are you waiting for? Open that laptop, fetch a notepad and a pen, and begin writing! Good luck!

And finally, if you liked the book, I would like to ask you to do me a favor and leave a review for the book on Amazon. Just go to your account on Amazon or click on the link below.

LEAVE A REVIEW ON AMAZON!

Thank you and good luck!

Printed in Great Britain
by Amazon

31329239R00018